OUR CLASSICAL HERITAGE

A HOMING DEVICE

Caroline Noble Whitbeck

To Dr. Galano,
with thanks! I hope your daughter enjoys it!
Carolin Whit

Winner of the 2006 Gatewood Prize
Selected by Arielle Greenberg

SWITCHBACK BOOKS
CHICAGO

ISBN-13: 978-0-9786172-1-9
ISBN-10: 0-9786172-1-5

LIBRARY OF CONGRESS CONTROL NUMBER: 2007923283

Book design: Cathy Nieciecki
Cover art: "Untitled, Boston." Photograph by Andrew Moisey.

Switchback Books
Brandi Homan, *Editor-in-Chief*
Hanna Andrews and Becca Klaver, *Founding Editors*
Kristin Aardsma, *Editor*
PO Box 478868
Chicago, IL 60647
editors@switchbackbooks.com
www.switchbackbooks.com

ACKNOWLEDGMENTS

Thank you to the editors of the following magazines where versions of some of these poems first appeared: *The Brown Literary Review, Cab/Net, Clerestory, Elimae, Horseless Review, Lumina,* and *Word For/Word.*

The author wishes to thank Brown University in general and the Literary Arts Department in particular for the chance to create this book. She also wishes to single out the following individuals for their help (inspiration, encouragement, contention, whatnot): C.D. Wright, Forrest Gander, Michael Tod Edgerton, Kate Schapira, Bronwen Tate, Lynn Xu, Michael Stewart, Tyler Carter, Erika Howsare, Jibade-Khalil Huffman, Adam Tobin, Jen Tynes, Brian Kim Stefans, Brianna Colburn, Michael Coppola, Ryan Daley, Nicole Dutton, Daniel Howe, Mike Kim, Brian Evenson, Gale Nelson, Elizabeth Brassil, Christine Schutt, Mary Stewart Hammond, Bear Kirkpatrick, Max Anderson, Seth Perlow, Andrew Moisey, Bob Berens, Eve Mayer, the *Budget Living* mafia, Alyssa Maloof, Bryan Rogers, Arielle Greenberg, the glorious Switchback editors, and, of course, her dear family, friends, former students, and bristly animal.

Sometimes, as young poets heeding Pound's dictum, we end up straining to make something strange in the service of novelty, rather than attempting to do that more difficult thing: to make it true. But when the poet comes along whose work is, from the first, strange and true and new at once, the reader has the sense that something is being dictated, to use Jack Spicer's word, from another realm, and to read such work is mystifying and also immensely satisfying. It is like witnessing an intimate and superb magic show. Such is the experience of reading Caroline Noble Whitbeck's *Our Classical Heritage: A Homing Device*.

Here is a book that wears its boldness loosely and lightly. As challenging as it is, *Our Classical Heritage* is a pleasurable and witty work, pinned sharply but delicately to reality through images of cultural detritus ("A cubic-zirconia also plus two baby birthstones heartshaped") and evocations of American childhood ("my / sister borrowed my gritty / glitterstick eyeliner / the unjangled / phone"). And despite its scope, *Our Classical Heritage* takes its time: it goes deep: "o / you. You sum. What / raw muscle wonder I wonder who / will make of you, / will you be / meat / or / music."

Caroline Noble Whitbeck offers fresh ways for a poem to function. These poems readjust expectations at the level of the word, in their ambitious and keen mix of dictions and sources (bouncing, for example, a "bolo tie" off of the "mouthblack summaries" a few poems later); of syntax, in their use of ecstatic exclamation buried by fracture ("See we are all generous untuck"); of the line, often interrupted, abridged or hyper-extended ("Have one sure so does the dog why bother what I come. I come."); of the sentence, which swings from pure lyricism to the beautiful exploitation of banal colloquialism ("Under the hairdryer's helmet, / their ruminant, that communal / consciousness, the consensus is."); and of the page, because these poems utilize traditional and avant-garde forms as well as the incorporation of multiple forms, and multiple poems, sometimes all on a single sheet.

It claims a "classical heritage," and seems concerned with piecing together the (invented?) fragmented language that serves as the poetic remains of the ancient world, often literally presented as the foundation of another poem, at the bottom of the page. But there is nothing fossilized here, nothing locked in amber: each page, each poem is fluid, present, and terribly alive. And the heritage it traces ranges from Pompey to the local trailer park, from Roman myth to the family estate. Of its poetic heritage, it seems to come out of nowhere and everywhere, out of the lineage of other visionaries: out of the ecstasy and everyday of Sappho and Spicer, out of the bloodied grin of C.D. Wright and Chelsey Minnis. But really, it doesn't sound like anyone else. Which is why I chose it.

One can wonder at what drives this book, but the force of the voice here is redoubtable. The world as described—"tinderbox, / hullabaloo"—may be a dizzying soup of existence, but Whitbeck can always locate herself: "I am my empty / home."

—Arielle Greenberg, March 2007

For my family and friends.
For my teachers.
For Bryan.

TABLE OF CONTENTS

CHOKECHERRY

May your beauty, blown umbrella.

In dreams each unholy closet opens.
A molotov christening, a surfeit of shitfans.
Your savor spoiling in an airless car.

May your devil-may-care, tenterhooks.

Green corridors of hopefulness unwind
onto hospital warrens, on every
swabbed rose the wreck of ethanol.

May your familiar, wet radio.

Night's dark cobblestep dogs you
home to your mother ringing your nerves'
lit tangle out in vinegar with the old lace.

May your blessings, back-combed.

In the mirror of your future, watch
your father puncture your instincts
on the machete-point of your friends.

May your puppy, oh flambé.

Let them come too early to infuse you
for the coffin. Your own name losing
its raw luck to the click.

This, my thumbprint on the mud:
May that black animal, upswell.

In Oklahoma I was the oven door your enamel the scattershot radio dial anything with a chrome handle. The manufacturer's initial. Waiting by the hotplate coil your lit wit in a hairnet. Here. Toing and froing the Airstream in your OTB absence. Waiting for my shift at the Superette the blip of the scanner. Okay.

Your pinkie tangled in my pin-curls at prom and ever since smoke rings.

I unspoon for the dog on the chain you keep. Maracas of kibble dishing out but pock up the still-wet lacquer. One toenail black from the oil drum. Your thumb inky from the betting pages. Tin box for the money. And thinner.

Little diet capsule with capsules inside swallow. Rattle.

That corner promised to the crib but the clinic said Wait. Kept the socks but balled the paper dress when the bill's in. Didn't warm it first gasp. We've got you covered sweaty palm sweetheart for once let me buy you one. Chocolate rose, foiled. And the wrapper too. Top bureau. Book of names for maybe.

Orange the Tupperware won't wash out reset the socket when the hairdryer.

The frozen peas do come in handy on employee discount. Rover's head otterwet picking ticks fat as. On the match and quick. Weeding among the engines on the lawn orb and gnome. Plastic pickets no space to swing but plenty for a skinned knee.

The checks of state for that first mistake Christmas card face known only.

Your mother in the Budweiser warmup peeling off bologna to the *Antiques Roadshow*. That's not worth it piece of junk I had a vase once. Picking through the racks for some new secondhand Rhoda has two school-aged so t-shirt with a dumptruck. I ring her up special. A cubic-zirconia also plus two baby birthstones heartshaped.

Bare velvet box windup ballerina sometime Ma lay off I mean it.

Greasestain on the chiffon from the pickup bed by the power plant bottleneck cough I'll show you a Big Dipper guffaw. Pass it will you wilting carnation. White ghost arc of the Wiffle ball socked between stuff of boys restless in rented-out. Girls older than their novelty IDs. All.

Sometimes I know I'm over scan the dailies opportunity gossip getaway car.

Would it be the same in Oregon in Ohio in Omaha in Olneyville elsewhere where there are openings left. Wonderment's trucker ribbon of urine tile threat and diner. Fleabag rumor. Sometimes I want to hang my hat to hitch. But such open such open. Or.

78   that ship's
      a hoary
      veteran

WINGS

The fret of the deal, that the

       wings were on. What nonchalance

earns, my cardigan sloughed. Apart, a dark

kitchen, a person's width,   coincidence

             wary between us, the luck. A freak

         purchase
            of self, little melting

      tether. You were the first

             to fillip the long, pooling what

whose night I no longer
noticed, or

    thought

        to name. Anyone.

             Dreamlack. The lake of it. I woke,

    little furrow across
      the mystery. I woke. You are going

home soon. Are not here

             in any sense that I can
                   say

    say "save." That I am

                 in. I am in.
              (Ahem,

              amen.)

      That I am my empty

      home.

79   denuded now

    but still
    satiety
    keeps

Solitary'll turn you sure they have computerized for a man of
your advanced in realworld clothes his manila packet of little
more. Circling and you could have been their own

trying

to remember what headlights the first hit lands. No stopping
these stretches should anything startle out with hands say
drive on citizen this one wore his sisters like women. Some

places

if you flush at once fuck the next round bring it toting no
birthday joke of what's baked in file says man I'd rather. Sure
I'll have done it if you'll do it to me they say cleaner.

80   [   ] in the ribs
                of the hold

Every man man his front porch every fat
pumpkin hollowed we will

swizzle this phantom thing this mist mongrel if it's
our last our last

Every man man his gun-turret every twitching
this is our trigger trick the nets

For days the stumps cauterized by
cold hell how on earth the cows too

I tell you man it's enough to empty
your eyes your eyes where your eyes

We have wood for the door the fire children
battened in the root cellar needs and tankards

The moon the moon in every last it rises the month
through wringing out lace hands the casement lock thrown

Another story cold on the sill
Courage men your collar

A witch nested in the wreck found news a cauldron maw
stew to make us squirm us hope through smoke

We boil rings for the silver plug bullets neat as
sin in the hand we make a marriage of it lift

the veil emptiness   Emptiness show us
your bleak visage your void view poison air

Hyphen where a scalp would hang your hairline your finest
feature fear

81 [   ] thus
    a fish
    skeleton
    across the plate

DUNE ROAD, 1941–2005

The summer
of blackout
shades and
mounted
police on
the beach
on
submarine
watch. Two
men
appeared
with crew
cuts and
blue jeans,
but
everyone
knew
everyone.
Where do
you live?

We came
daily for
the paper
and one
candy
apiece;
they
returned to
their limp
raft and
were ----------

```
----------------
----------were-
----------------
--were--------
----------------
----------------
----------------
-----waves-----
```

From   this
strand   most
days   you
can   still
see   boats
grappling
for
airliners
or   simpler
fish.

82   [she] returns her men
      on the tide

THE WAR HERO

Later we had to kill him (*captain come to the surface*) we'd torpedoed (*the only survivor*) for weeks I interrogated until the smell (*whatsis*) he'd hoarded butter rotten (*but this is America*) letters came in code so she'd have his coordinates (*baby*) the enemy'd be on the beaches with forks and knives (*what we did was necessary*) ash in the anti-aircraft shells for years he worked for the home machine (*genealogies*) saving you the second helping

AMNESIA

(*From scudding in the shower*) watching the orderly scissor the stitches open
weeks after the wound had unknit (*wife with the dishtowel*) hands flapping
before him counting off (*thank god for this bounty*) today he woke with a new
bracelet a new name saying it gets so late so early nowadays that's not
what I mean dark (*I mean dark*) where is his (*faceless*) waiting to wake him
to their voices (*we're here we're all here*) please it's so hard to place

LISTEN & RESPOND FROM ANY PHONE

LOCAL MORNING EDITION

TEENAGERS STAR IN THE STORY OF THEIR LIVES, PAINFUL DETAILS AND ALL

Slim Fits one hand under
the hem my blister shoes my
sister borrowed my gritty
glitterstick eyeliner the unjangled
phone our mother made us
matching set garnet
birthstone Cancun
photo shot
glasses yup
plastic
twofer
a
backlit
yearbook
scrawl stuffed hound
abed with
the balled slamnote
scrutiny steam the
bathroom aplomb doleful
my Adderall my adorable rub
of Jansport rote locker
territorialities
excelsior cancer

SEX, ENVY, PROXIMITY

Readiness in the clan. To cross the grass on wet stockings.
The blade freighted with sugar, ablation. The bridal
bite. Long dun column through an upstairs room.

Younger sister at the portal. What is touching now.
Applause of the wash. To hide, the netted candy hot in hand.
To watch, the machine. Bladders of milk folded in.

SEE DADDY MAKE A DEAL

At the bank I've been
trying nights when the pipes
knock that's the heat
coming on.

Heat's schooling

due the wind jellies windows across
the way I let the hand-dryer
sink in too long timetables away from
my voluble home

the dinner scum

done. I will the microwaves full
frontal at the hum this unplated
wet this phoned-in
vegetable

rim. Sleepyheads you know only

my unrinsed breakfast
glass of half-full all
day waiting. Go in and
kiss them visitor suited

up. Man on the rung.

THEY'RE ALL OUT OF STORM NAMES

Because he'd been *cleaning the gun*, she brought a leash to school.
Because it was attached to nothing, like accident.

At the cubbies, she unfurled to show me, and I
licked her palm. You know, she said. You have one too.

What did I know? I'd learned to let another girl
tie my shoes for me, sure. What else is there, my parents asked.

At home, the bitch writhed as she
buried her hands in. I'll bet you're hungry, she said to the teeth.

WHAT TO DO IF YOUR KID IS A BULLY

Livid like her

plastic kit of
not-leaving-this-house, strap

a beefsteak to that, throw a

trainwreck. Hands
down where the money is these

days. Hitting home we live

here sorry. Which makes me
page through this mess of

names daily. The little

assurances it goes on. It
goes on. There'll be

others

when I'm gone. Down
swinging grin

here son.

This life's a leg of
poison so

survive. Say suck on.

OUR LADY OF THE MAXI-PAD

Lost it (*later his baby*) to a boy broke dates to write thank-you notes (*in through the window*) a cinderblock basement hum of vending and ruminant laundry girls breathing the bathroom Glade (*cruiser brought them home*) even with the shaved head (*mock icon*) she had your face taped up (*and paisley wash*) to laugh at the weave seeing what in the (*congratulation cycles*) no use now (*to punch your coins in jam the lockdown*) God your green green lungs

KEEP HANDS FREE WHEN IN MOTION

There was a dish (*childhood*) spoon until you see the smile (*under*) all
cinderblock and poster years from the same (*wishful*) when the hotel room
(*finally*) hotwire but no blood (*years of horseback*) you packet of pills
congratulations go buy a taxi at the surcharge hours (*streets hosed*) mine
warm homegoing but when it breaks a succession (*oh success*) cache of
Thanksgiving placecards saving (*the biopsy site*) the surgeon said lean on it

CLEEK

Once again, arable. Awake to tensions
rooting through: Distractibility's

cattail wag. Bits that wayside and cleave.
The window's heat-lamp of what-ifs, a rictus

of awe (read: hunger with nothing
hung on). These, my clock tines, my ribsy

evenings. I would like to cobble together
a pittance, so green, so good, to keep, for you.

Afraid of the fraud of my wonderment, its
staleness (tick, tick). The littles that become

whether you're watching or elsewhere. The aposiopetic
brushpopper eyes the thorough-going

rabbit: Palmable myth. Warm animal
of home-feeling, alive in the thrum. Even you

house the wicked, insensate No. (A bit of lead
can coax out). Chew thoughtfully, thing, you're on.

73   to the bluffs

All day the birds
annotate

the window, your daily
dream of

attention.
The heat is

real,
the sidewalks rote.

There is voltage,
trash, and

in-betweenness
to skirt. Carry your own

storm
over reservoir, the joggers'

clockwork,
the busying rim. Unpack

your prayer to
unlatch.

Soon sleep will.
Riding

the rails.
Hello

hello now
to the breathing

vestibule. The
icebox

hum. Water
runs, what

sustains.
Anything

to find them
so

suitable for
framing. *Home*

now.
Even this.

Each *mother*
please. The bolo tie scuds

down. Please stab
at pale,

ordinary
vegetables in the

TV dark, please roll
the blind

thunder down, family
battening down

the night, buttoning
up.

65 places where
elephants
sport minor
cities
on their backs

The living will congregate. Thing is.

The living will cup their hands or wring them. Animal, vegetable,
mineral, vessel, pick one.

The living will do this thing with water. To weather an arrest or
a new name.

The living will debate the disobedient. The homonyms holy and wholly.

The living will run cover headlines ENOUGH. Really? They will

talk about love. Where on the face does the soul
enter?

The living will wait for the updates. Help me, nurse, to change
this bed I never knew I could.

I will tell their friends, the living, "No, not yet." The definition of
echolocation: I am here, you are here, ocean.

56 decamped in the
grasses packing
a comrade's
wound with mud and
leather

at dawn [it] yellows

The stomacher can only
staunch so much. Moansong

of leeches under linen and
herbaceous molder rising from the

poultice. Peel the wax
from the cask to wash clean

the *unspeakable*. (Rustle
in the corridor suspects:

handsaw.) Tallow scent of snuffed
flame. After the voices

cauterize, we resume our
glassine stations [*see also:*

Ankyloglossia]: attention,
furniture, minstrel, cauldron, coffin, lookout.

47 five days past
the last finger
of land visible

oar-men
chew their blister-skin

Finger the seams, cathexis

of readiness and need, the knot in the unseen harness. Bundled, a house he
won't shrug on. Those thresholds cordoning off requitement.

I nick it a little.

The storied well, the room I am always in. This inevitable his grafted red
has ceased to hold. A hand in the boiling pot, it

lifts. After one silence smaller,

the little hiccup, the soughing door. All hooks uprooted. Such dreams carry
the incendiary animals, transit. I would give anything for that

scorched laughter.

Because we had torched the library, I mean. Our mouthblack summaries, the
weird weather of our kindness, the newly stripped wind: I

don't like it either. Keep on, new coat. You too.

43   salt nausea
     [   ] Cormorant

INHERITANCE

INHERITANCE

A DAUGHTER

HER LOVER

HER MOTHER

HER FATHER

that there is liquid to a "girl,"
a low growl of letters, like the rut of a sewing machine.

The rest is raw, is
gigging.

Like any liquid, she will
ravel. The tic—bright girl!—to arterial blood, the water

ruffled on rock.
Will run

backwards. Will run, a
contrarian, cowlick. What won't lie flat on the forehead,

future, inscrutable page. No matter what,
run, mother
thumb

THIS MESS.

"The end depends upon the beginning."

—Manlius

INHERITANCE, A DAUGHTER

Already, now,

a daughter, her lover, her mother.

A two-room, the lip of lake, the
rowboat dragged to dry and a crop of
spare parts. Nothing so fallow.
Road so long the postman
won't. The walk they take
to fetch what is owed.

"A bow is alive only when it kills."

—Herakleitos

INHERITANCE

Was a hands-on marriage new name keyed in over the heirloom. For first
love bundling home pale fingerlings in flannel at the belly still warm
when I laid the knife in. Wet hanks far as the clavicle but who'd laugh.
Could trawl that farther.

You can work a wan thing in any light
I learn. Hands quick unfasten him the animal now *death they don't
know it poor wights* is my mother stirring idly. Turpentine on all her
silverplated place she knows better than to sit without a cushion down I
nick a half-smoked off the floor hook one finger in his navel sleeping tell
her none of this. Goldtone gasket anyone would confuse for. Tell her try.
She'll leave but not her rose for hours.

He comes with an oarlock and a strop stopping just *Mother*
wait for me to rinse his *left money*. Seeding salvage to the spoonclean
mayonnaise were never *savages* when we decide to it is her pillow we
will use.

Why I wed. What he commits.

Out of what wooded boyhood did I startle that he

*Where does your hunger bunk and who keeps it
who slips in alongside?*

Like laundry from the line
wrested loose say just the
night dragging its skirts is.
All her rings fit.

See we are all generous untuck and taking
his hangnail in teeth feeding it to him I am so suddenly grown.

KILLICK, HER LOVER

And earlier,

her lover finds her.

"You want to?" she asked.
He was mute, animal.

"You want to," she said,

guiding his hand.

KILLICK

Have one sure so does the dog why bother what I come. I come.

Swung through by my fingernails
the lintels my initials soldered on the dog-door banging behind *hey
home.*

What I've fingered from the pay phone. What's been palmed at the last
gas soup packets antacids such blue satin roses across the oil cloth
squirrel away hers.

A safety blade. Its notched ease
what it means. To hold.

Found her first squatting behind the dumpster a pinned toad and a
scauper let me decide. Hand on the twitch her steady. Let her swab off
my own bib after.

After. Home to unplank the swingset for hope chest or
tinder finding her own hewn taglock wadded in back pocket. To suck on.

Nights. Listen. Night falls through like a depth charge. Through water.

Here nosing the sheers aside wag *what's at the feeder
boy* see. She. On the property line creek up to her knees
to gig frisson the moon.

A snail-trail of fractured wet. Green I fold into her impress home.

A rowboat a pastel postcard since I've been shoring up to the lozenge box living on unstuck from plastic wrap. Little boiled. Taken to bringing her cigar boxes tacked in bringing them *lift the lid* she lifts. She calls me down the chainlink calls me her breath on my nape a mother. Little white neighborhood kicks in its ether.

GRAVID, HER MOTHER

Earlier, ever earlier

her mother, who knows what she carries.

Her mother's friends, their flowers, their
chafing dishes. And worry. A blister pack of pills.
What such talk does over spoonfuls of
coffee whitener. What condolence becomes
beyond the ear of the eaves.

Was it not his? What did he

know? Was it true he'd tried to
swaddle his head in her old

nightgown before, that is,

(trigger with the finger).

Under the hairdryer's helmet,
their ruminant, that communal
consciousness, the consensus is.
Her doleful shoals. Her money, her cloister,
her narrow window through which. His necessary.

Months now, local children set a bounty on touching
the car wherein.

That she might be watching. Their giddy

scatter. Impossible
laughter, dusting away.

None suspect her own laughter Was it

laughter,
doctor.

Doctor?

GRAVID

Feel that.

       He was she was.

Tender as worms in and

                     blind. I know. Ruin. Run a fork tine
along the veins in hand the waiting.

                         Little blue thrum.

   Is there what isn't what won't fit anymore the keeping. My silk
pouch swaddled in my sleeping things sachet my
irreducible my oyster.

           Comb on the nightstand anymore.

             His smell is in it his hair still what won't
lift from the driverside and still I won't sell. The brilliantined
attorneys. The pen lifted leaking my eye
on the nib its

                 wicked split enunciating *done*. Who drives.
Now *order is in everything*.

               Gentlemen.

To tip and leave I

             lock up after and inhabit. Unplate
what is brought inevitable eat eaten. What is
expected. Grows.

                Even as I run the knife along upkeep
is so purposed she. Will come.

       Swallow to swallow. His rigged

fit has seen to his other trigger his after.

                          To bring back the man

dragging through her on her my own sown making my own

story my surplus.

           Like salt through water stirs. Through. My bodied

        waiting. Sit now. What this

is and is for anyone under the light of it

why fight. What we

         know due tuck in say *swallow*.

             This lungful. Is said

of this. Lift the receiver from the cradle.

           Mum. I am. *Hello*. The sudden the

night runs naked through.

                Rutting toddler.

                Unchastened.

HOMECOMING, HER FATHER

So it begins, her

father, mother.

What it

takes.   You can

depend.

HOMECOMING

Lady your mantle wordlessly

    your years now. Buttons thumbed

   through their slits.

  Sullen combed.

My handle was familiar I wore

     the smell of your sleep its deep pond

primitive the imperatives

   from your prayers their lace their lifted lid. Parole.

 Little

   lock of home leaving is what we do

 we know daily. But to *wife*

     to live as. Doublebent as a snail.

     I rub and rub and yet the red

  in the chamberpot's waters I rinse diligent.

Mornings you manage your seething

remedy. My comfort

     the cold coffee colder clocks.

     That the wallpaper curls.

  A dailiness I decide. What I decide.

I have walked again to the sink but

cannot.

                              My black drive

                              idles just outside the hedgerow prim

            as your sex.

            What I will do.

            I will make you a promise.

Blond in my teeth, the coat's weave, weeks now. Waking one end of the Brooklyn walk-up. The susurrating curtains stained dawn. Odd bread and

dilute juice breakfast. Open my door and his light blanked on. Stereo backdrop. Japanese cigarettes stacked in the kitchen with the dishes and the

robot stuff of boys. Afternoons the intercom's radar eye was mine, the street a goggled soundstage of green wind reenacting the world.

The occasional comma of a person, that lit tip, his rules: One must leave one's boots at the door. Stepping out of my days, I slept in unwashed smoke,

ours. Chew the guitar-strings of his, hair and bracelets. The insect-view of an armpit's forest. Mascara clotted under each. Alike.

At home only in the mirror together, ropey wet and not much beyond that shine. Even so I rubbed on rank clothes, smug in my publicly smelling his

young barnyard on me. Wanton indelible, that doleful wag. Not-a-thumb in my back mornings: Master Me, Take Me Out.

32 first the wooden sword
    tilting at hay-bales

    the girls plait myrtle
    preparing mock-laurels
    for the victor

Check the box, subject
can still sleep, isn't

eating fragments. The flannel stuff
of local waitfulness

worn in. I am home where
my mole warms. Tinderbox,

hullabaloo. The dog nosing
pillows of unconcern, hi Mom. And now

my importance is due. I find
what, outpacking the shells and sundry

appointments: you and yours. Your skull
I bunk with, on the watch. Mock up my day

book, spooning fungible
anything toward my face, where

I wore it. Batty old
driving horn, noisenoise. I am so

sorry I can say nothing more
consoling to you for love in action is

a story we each. Halve
this guiltshare, the erotics

of difference, an unskilled
comma between us curling. A fetal thing

the world is nowadays, the rub. Greats and
ancients: You are in

your book. I am
chain-smoking. There is razor

wire it is out there what
to be done. The what hum. Our pet

debate. Should I
simmer? What mouth is left? Skulking, my

pot for weeks, me. Over the
phone they tell me they're here.

33 [   ] fresh
the dew was still on

[   ] wet about the head

This marble has veins, this brick pitted like
skin. Oh my
goblin, don your saddle shoes. Go

coat your claws in stop-red lacquer. Strop them.
Centuries
unfurl stinking of schoolgirl wool,

chalk dust, origin of the older stars,
pore of bone.
Cross-section of her raw humor:

Adolescens, adolescentis. (Note:
for *girl* see
also: guile, brittle, leak, and loom.)

Caesura in the air, tuning mortal
radio:
ambulance soprano. Doctor's

black bag with its hushlock: "Love Is Strong As
Death." As Death
what? (The copse keeping mum.) What now.

22   the shadow
of Mount Helicon
[liquid]

What was I after
in the orchard the
roots What was the lesson
he missed the rhetoric And
on the bed the eiderdown
And on the plate the urgency
the peat the impossibilities What
was the string that snapped the golden
plectrum the bedpan the syllables
an unstrung a bowl of unripe
the rinds the bracelet the bare wrist

23 Artemis

    your untouched
    acolyte
    no
    more

AS ALWAYS ON ELM STREET

After your skittish key scratch (*car alarm furled*) a nervous rain's savor
(*cumulus unwoven in broth*) say girly'll be safe here the wind unhinges
(*locket script*) the quilt outpacked (*a nipped tin scent*) remember Daddy's
army buddy a Yours Truly blade thin (*the bluing poollight*) as you batten
down the basement footfalls (*bass notes*) those tentatus hands raking the
latch outback (*what motor purr*) now operator I'll carve mine

THE MOP LADY

Panting back hall is that her (*door and bucket angle*) where a face would fantasize (*her fire extinguisher*) her recognition (*giggle*) by the exit lights (*likely alarmed*) to dream her stagger scatter the cop car (*incoming*) halogen and terrarium tick (*the knee wincing cold*) that rubber strap chain in hand (*an ember on one blue finger*) huffing home the bleacher ribs (*old dinosaur teacher*) not to smell the (*night liberty*) smoke on wool on you hers

The air of *there are*, the feeling
of people doing things. Mere, the mirror.

The sobs that bark, the house that hums, you
with? By starlight my everyone glows. Oh there

are no stars. Gas lamps of an antique. You lovelorn
lineup of carnival ducks: Spun, hit, tin riddled

"thin as a repeated dream." This is my last,
jangled chance, precipice of sameness, as another

racks up. I hang up the rag. Little dustlessness,
wreck of industry, indelible wanting, bloodwarm.

For a spell you kept your shoes here. A house
like any other. Warm lozenge of window, suckle.

Muddled stories' green scent on the stove where
I know nothing else. Beckon with a bell my

obsequy. This is the sky today, the gimmick.
Neighbors, I stand naked at the prow, isn't this

my swath? Cold and it is hitting. Scent of
time in a vial. Ozone, a concerto, baby alien:

What we send, we are alive, we rare. Wound
miracle for what it's worth no matter where

the spotlight wends concentric. Indiscriminate,
unwashed *enfant*, I-love-you device, come home.

17   hip-high in the clover
     [   ] bundle him

NOOSPHERE

AN ARS POETICA

"But what is more interesting ... is that *information itself*—the materialization and amplification of human spirit in streams of data—*might now be considered a force of nature.*"

—Ando Arike, *Harper's Magazine,* January 2006

*

The name of God is in the world like any
other object. Even *table* and *blunderbuss*

share its retinue. The implacable soughing
trees trees. Ours. Our grout and

bristle. Our children and their
thumbable faces. Whitened tilted

up. What can they want of us?
Cloud trenchant calico humbug.

We speak in advent
to that dog whistle. It wags us each

unflagging effort a welling forth.
A bloodwet instinct

to noun

to nurse.

*

And so everything ever read is
true enough nothing

to button a sweater about. *Desuetude*
confused for *desire* but for

the shapes it takes everyone
recognizes a man on all fours.

Furcula who still recalls
the split for luck the girl

fingering what novel slack the verb is
near indistinguishable *to go*

around to survive: Onto the
pack heap

hay bales round the parish house
leeward.

*

What story is older than is other than
looking. And I have no answers

besides this: he leaves
she's left to account her valuables.

What was I looking for in that
book? All these years. I sing the same

with my eyes closed your
ellipsis. *Anymore.* The world is

in such things patient
as a window and as

generous. *I want this for anyone else*
is a form of love. Only the pronouns

change. Moving through the mind like others.
Keeping company.

I.

Sin riding teen cars: Obit.
Keep or lose.

O not old or
do not lean, o door!

II.

Vacation,
do not exit. Tan less.

Diet to do so,
tin crew.

O men, O low strut.

Ire and mere work.

III.

Merge it.

Pull and rove, rube. Mercy
in: Window real.

Ate rest. Hand on now.
And u had wars, u use red.

Had to trip away, rub old
late meal, hale. On, win, and

pull: Tow, you, O!
Move in pan.

8   the water [already]
     runs
     through the wood

     [   ] its quick grain

It won't cause drowsiness—you can drive.

"Past the children living in
Poverty,"
   a refrigerator-
   sized box

bruised with juices and
postal codes. They have

lost their shoes to the telephone
poles and overhead wires.
      Their appetites

patter on the tar-pocked roofs alighting
pigeons. No, that isn't rain, that's
   Miss Prison.

Around here, she wears a red-laser spot on her neck.

In the dark, someone
emptied out the drawers, tacked everything
to a white sheet and ran the tape.
      You can

cut through anything with this here.

     Lovingly
     handcrafted, you
get a full set.

Fortified with
siding,
shingles,
sandal rubber,
vitamin
   circulars when the board ceded to
   mold and teeth. We are ready

to take your order, but
is it right for your kind of pain?

An offscreen
hand halves a can, lets the
      contents ooze.

This is all I've had today.

9   springy
      under the ship-builder's
      mallet

A MUSEUM LOCATED IN THE MIND OF ITS DIRECTOR

If you were a statue love I'd throw a party your arms off I

haunt the plangent halls heels on swizzlethin women of a

certain chisel each one ruttable Classical placards upending palate

upon wet palate my peerless archetype Parian auction

winnings what shucked exit tickets could requite my venal

plated reproduction bracelet oh you

docent you dove-cote prioress you

priceless coo you pyramidal

long cool view

11   his hand along the contours
     [   ] their course

LADY LUCK

The Singer ceded to skin, Mother, chiffon wash
of swabbed-up, what pools, indelible, bundles
wedded to the needlebar. 'Nother mural goes to town.
Out here a shot-bottle will, in a trade. [*At the
footlight*s] Wanna try? Isn't a feather; doesn't
tickle.

Was underground, for a while. Knew whose
mailbox to bark at. My first? Cigarette ground
for cinder, the sharp steadied on a
matchstick, prison-style. Cut the umbilical
myself! [*Laughter*] Not that school, not the
dancing kind.

Oh "property of," no. No putty rolled in
newsprint, no sticker-licking baby, dunno.
What collects: Facts, rockcandy surfaces of
Perspex, dust-rinsed Hummels. [*Sound of the
drill*] Of course. Hum of my venal, teeth of
my plastic grass, oh my welcome words.

Risible roses, big-tittied atomic bombs, to
each his own hewn. Outside, the clientele pump
coins into. Anoint, this practice of healing
appreciates. Ribbon threaded where the wound;
blood, we've found something strong as.
[*Curtain of clothing, lifts*]

Not all start as but sometimes the chicken heh
heh wants his neck. This wrist exacts, things wince,
the chain on the chopper, or. Hon I'm your color
once the tender sheds [*Hand along the outstep*].
Here, when I'd enough potatoes I'd inked.
How those juices wear.

Course canning wasn't enough. Things to hock.
[*Hand up*] Hair, believe it. To soothe I thought
things I could. Barber-tonic blue. Even neon
for the shingle? Yeah, but home and that's when
I lost. Helmet hit me where. Why I won't
do names, only covers.

The biggest dog, you know, needs
the hose? Yes since. Cardigan government
woman, pfft. Milk, carrot sticks, homework,
happy? Just because it bleeds I mean. My sheets
white really. Machine runs. Who put those
pearls through her, wonder [*Hand comes from ear, red*].

Tell you, it keeps the peanut butter,
keeps in flea collar, turns the dimmer,
bides. Legend for the bedside, braille better
than any breadcrumb where the bled-out. That
was the practice and this [*Gauze
goes, motherglove, hush.*]

12 encouragement
[   ] a nail

Memorizing new rooms, blind footprint the eager
sleeper would. When will I stop

crossing each threshold with
the home wish. If I

could enter an evening the way one enters a
vestibule of work. Filaments

above a dark street instead an unfiring. Weak fret of
masturbation doesn't. Relent runs

west with the traffic night runnel. This is petty what, my
passage: skin weight compass a pot on. I could

so much I don't rip ask anyone. Here is soft
habit gesture

history spilt to put you in yours. A person
in place a placated. My name

in your mouth please, feed. Walking back the raw
erotic starts, an early

blood. Is it wrong to want
to save for you

the feel of seething
water.

1   on Helicon
     the
     stands

     [   ] trees hiss

     the sound
     of the ax

     its pulse

     [   ] yet
     far off

O

the socket let the word in.

Let it world it.
Birthing opposites and old friends.

Linkages
a trick to spin on your finger, the

quarter on the rim—

and off.

The trick with people is

is

loneliness. I am not

afraid to lean on it
or am, but

the wearing

the wearing it out—.

What I have that does
or

doesn't match, how
welcome wanes. A threshhold where

the lock gets thrown (you

say lock I hear locket).
This game

has centuries stacked through it like
a roll of coins, clean

in a sleeve. Bank on nothing.

I did not get
in my exchange

what I gave: My gold. My golden gift for it.

There was something familiar in the going,
though.

A toughness

I thought I'd
chewed
through.

Years and the old jaw
grows sore. Words,

spending.

Such
thrift as I'd never o

you. You sum. What

raw muscle wonder I wonder who
will make of you,

will you be
meat
or
music

when the time comes to change, to change it in: Your
turn: Love

like something
                    thrown
                from the nest

here.   I used to rest my head here

                            now I want

                            to rest my head

simply.

To tarry.
Entirely.

            Open again and all. The tally of awe
            by all accounts coming out ahead.

                        The even keel of keeping.

2 [   ] mother
  land of light

COLOPHON

Nights in the blue house the (*shape of*) windows careful to live it by what (*homing*) comes the streetlight I learn rain or snow through a fingerthicket of blinds can I see (*you*) you have seen me undressed but stepping from the coverlet with my babyhairs (*hope*) raised white by the outside motion trips it feeling in the dark for the (*trigger*) remembering suddenly the mundane standing the frozen aisle where I once lived (*my basket*) holding and eyes on

OUR CLASSICAL HERITAGE
an apparatus criticus

I.
The lake in the text. Wet footprint left
by the unshod instep. Now gird
yourself and keep going.

Ed. Note: Dubious attribution. See also: Naumachiae.

II.
Is a question of derivation. Rattle-dry
seedpods of meaning. For instance: Phylactery
and lactate. Martyrs leaking blood but never
milk. Is a question of what [   ]
to keep, it keeps, in keeping
[   ]
[   ]
tractability, [   ] urn

III.
patior, uror, verberor, interficior;
harena. The difference between dust
and sand: grit. Catena–catena–catena–
–catena– et cetera. Into the other –rum.

IV.
Homophones, such as scarcely, I lived,
vetch, to the village, I conquered,
change/interchange. Also: pyre and I ask.

V.
Ed. Note: Codex Alpha was discovered
in an urn; Codex Beta in the mortar
of a barn; Codex Gamma plastered
to a mummy's instep.

VI.
[   ] the head and hands,
and [   ] on a pike [ ] basket,
[   ] Cicero and Pompey respectively

VII.
Amphora, Pegasus, apples of gold, wine
stirred with honey or left sediment-thick.

The scalpel precision of hamstrung.
Even that. Even the fat, quivering spear.

VIII.
Theshewolfthewhelpsthewildernessachingtonurse

IX.
Paraleipsis: a choreographed heel
scudding down the stair. The bailiff: "All
swivel!" The rhetorician
coughs over his chuckle,
missing nothing. And, turning to
the Forum, he begins:

"Citizens," he says.

In "Inheritance," the Manlius quotation is the author's own translati[on] (and high school motto); the Herakleitos quotation is Guy Davenport['s] translation from his anthology 7 *Greeks*.

In "Send More," the quotation "sorry I can say nothing more / consol[e] to you for love in action is" is taken from the translation of Fyodor Dostoyevsky's *The Brothers Karamazov* cited in Hal Hartley's film *Surviving Desire*.

The following titles were taken from aol.com, msn.com, and nytimes.com home page headlines from roughly a two-week period during the fall of 2005: "When It's Easier to Play Older, Wiser, Wearier," "Listen and Respond From Any Phone, Local Morning Edition," "Teenagers Star in the Story of Their Lives, Painful Details and All," "Sex, Envy, Proximity," "See Daddy Make a Deal," "They're All Out of Storm Names," "What To Do if Your Kid Is a Bully," and "A Museum Located in the Mind of Its Director."

on

's

ng